Lowercase Letters

Writing c

Name

Date

W9-ATK-451

■ Say the sound of the letter as you trace it. Then read the words aloud, and say the sound of the first letter as you trace it.

To parents

On the following pages, your child will learn cursive lowercase letters. Before your child begins writing the first letter of the words, please ask him or her to read the words on the page. Encourage your child to write the letters carefully and say the sound of the letter aloud while he or she traces it. When your child completes each exercise, praise him or her.

c ▶ c

can

coat

can

coat

can

coat

Writing *a*

■ Say the sound of the letter as you trace it. Then read the words aloud, and say the sound of the first letter as you trace it.

ant

apple

ant

apple

ant

apple

Lowercase Letters

Writing *g*

Name

Date

■ Say the sound of the letter as you trace it. Then read the words aloud, and say the sound of the first letter as you trace it.

To parents
Do not be concerned if your child cannot write the letters perfectly at first. He or she will gradually be able to do so after repeated practice. When your child is finished, offer praise, such as, "Nice work!"

g ▸ *g*

g ▸ *g* ▸ *g* ▸ *g* ▸ *g*

gum

goat

gum

goat

gum

goat

Review   Writing *c*, *a*, and *g*

■Read the words aloud, then say the sound of the letter as you trace it.

can
can

ant
ant

gum
gum

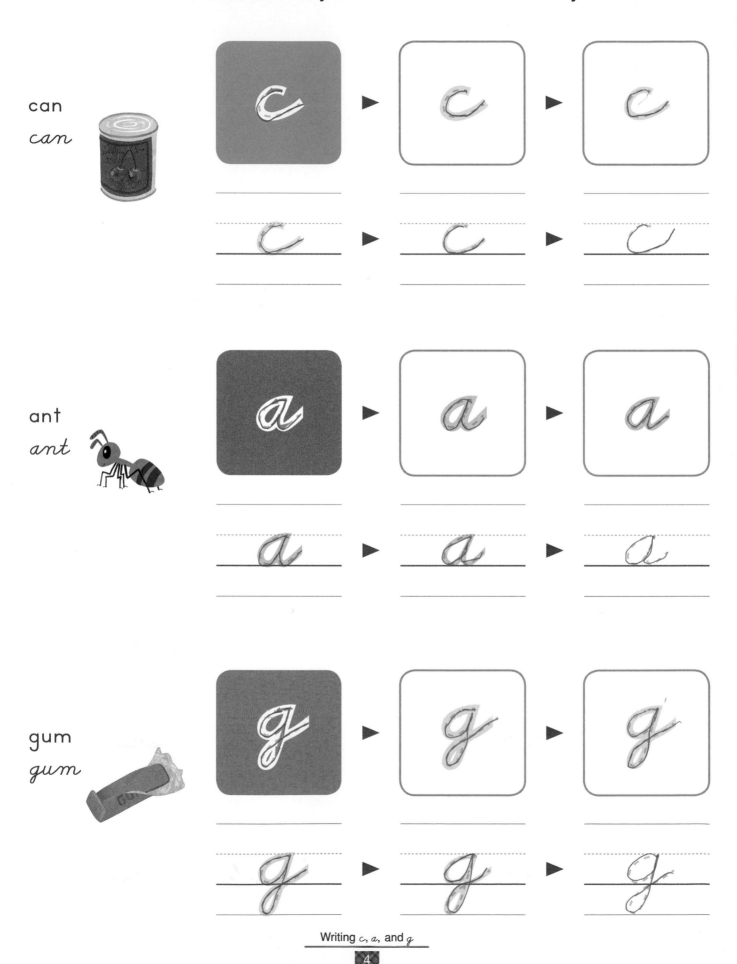

3 Lowercase Letters

Writing *o*

■ Say the sound of the letter as you trace it. Then read the words aloud, and say the sound of the first letter as you trace it.

O ▶ o

ox

octopus

ox   octopus

ox   octopus

Writing *d*

■Say the sound of the letter as you trace it. Then read the words aloud,
 and say the sound of the first letter as you trace it.

doll

dog

Lowercase Letters

Writing *q*

■ Say the sound of the letter as you trace it. Then read the words aloud, and say the sound of the first letter as you trace it.

q ▸ *q*

quail

queen

quail

queen

quail

queen

Review Writing *o*, *d*, and *q*

■Read the words aloud, then say the sound of the letter as you trace it.

ox
ox

doll
doll

quail
quail

Name

Date

■Say the sound of the letter as you trace it. Then read the words aloud, and say the sound of the first letter as you trace it.

lemon

lamp

Writing *e*

■ Say the sound of the letter as you trace it. Then read the words aloud, and say the sound of the first letter as you trace it.

egg

elephant

egg

lephant

egg

lephant

Lowercase Letters

Writing *f*

■ Say the sound of the letter as you trace it. Then read the words aloud, and say the sound of the first letter as you trace it.

flute

flag

flute

flag

lute

lag

Review Writing *l*, *e*, and *f*

■ Read the words aloud, then say the sound of the letter as you trace it.

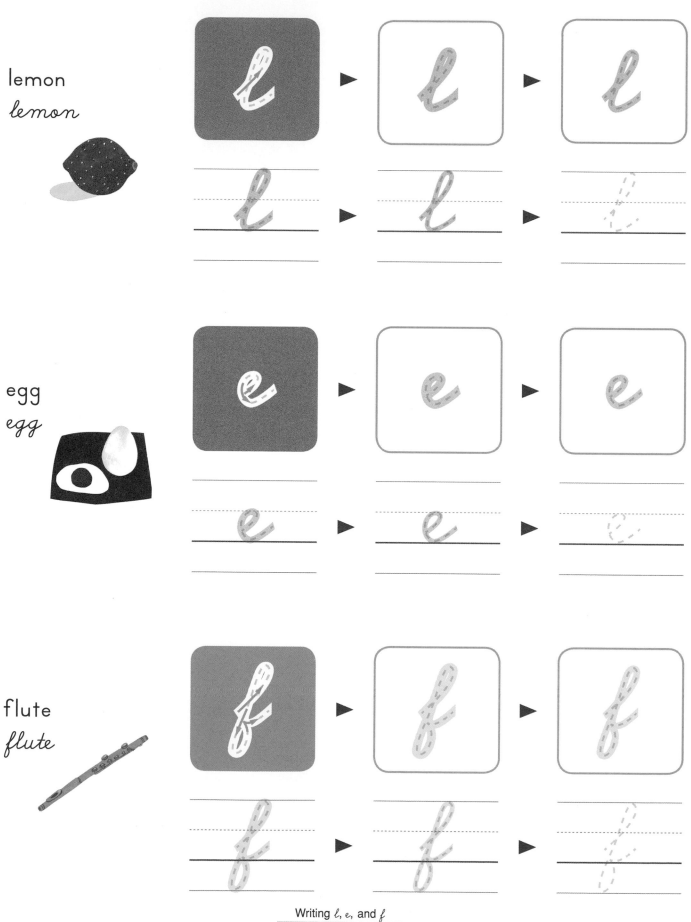

lemon
lemon

egg
egg

flute
flute

Name

Date

■Say the sound of the letter as you trace it. Then read the words aloud, and say the sound of the first letter as you trace it.

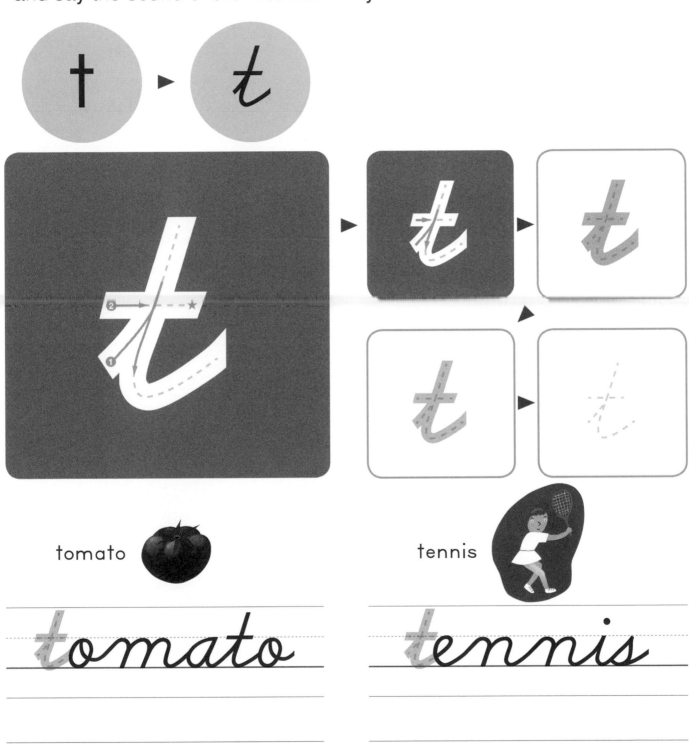

tomato

tennis

tomato

tennis

tomato

tennis

Writing _i_

■ Say the sound of the letter as you trace it. Then read the words aloud, and say the sound of the first letter as you trace it.

iguana

iguana

guana

ink

ink

nk

Lowercase Letters

Writing u

■ Say the sound of the letter as you trace it. Then read the words aloud, and say the sound of the first letter as you trace it.

u ▶ u

up

unicorn

up

up

unicorn

nicorn

Review Writing *t*, *i*, and *u*

■ Read the words aloud, then say the sound of the letter as you trace it.

tomato
tomato

iguana
iguana

up
up

Lowercase Letters

Writing w

Name	
Date	

To parents
Now your child will begin learning more complex letter shapes. If your child encounters difficulty, encourage him or her to write slowly and follow the tracing lines closely. Offer your child lots of praise when he or she finishes each exercise.

■ Say the sound of the letter as you trace it. Then read the words aloud, and say the sound of the first letter as you trace it.

w ▶ w

wink

$wink$

ink

wet

wet

et

Writing *j*

■ Say the sound of the letter as you trace it. Then read the words aloud, and say the sound of the first letter as you trace it.

jacket

jacket

acket

jump

jump

ump

Lowercase Letters

Writing *y*

■ Say the sound of the letter as you trace it. Then read the words aloud, and say the sound of the first letter as you trace it.

yak

yum

Review Writing *w*, *j*, and *y*

■Read the words aloud, then say the sound of the letter as you trace it.

wink
wink

jacket
jacket

yak
yak

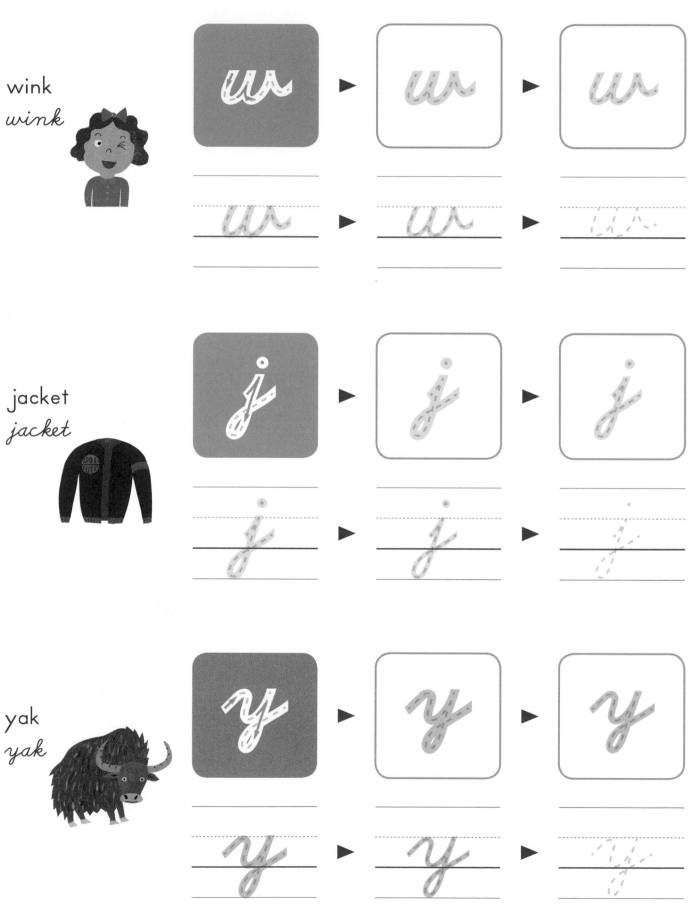

Lowercase Letters

Writing *h*

Name

Date

■ Say the sound of the letter as you trace it. Then read the words aloud, and say the sound of the first letter as you trace it.

h ▶ *h*

h ▶ *h* ▶ *h*

h ▶ *h*

hippo

hose

hippo

hose

hippo

hose

Writing *k*

■ Say the sound of the letter as you trace it. Then read the words aloud, and say the sound of the first letter as you trace it.

kite

knee

Lowercase Letters

Writing *p*

■ Say the sound of the letter as you trace it. Then read the words aloud, and say the sound of the first letter as you trace it.

plane

panda

plane

panda

lane

anda

Review Writing *h*, *k*, and *p*

■Read the words aloud, then say the sound of the letter as you trace it.

hippo
hippo

kite
kite

plane
plane

Lowercase Letters
Writing *b*

■ Say the sound of the letter as you trace it. Then read the words aloud, and say the sound of the first letter as you trace it.

b ▶ *b*

bat

bag

bat

bat

bag

bag

Writing *s*

■Say the sound of the letter as you trace it. Then read the words aloud, and say the sound of the first letter as you trace it.

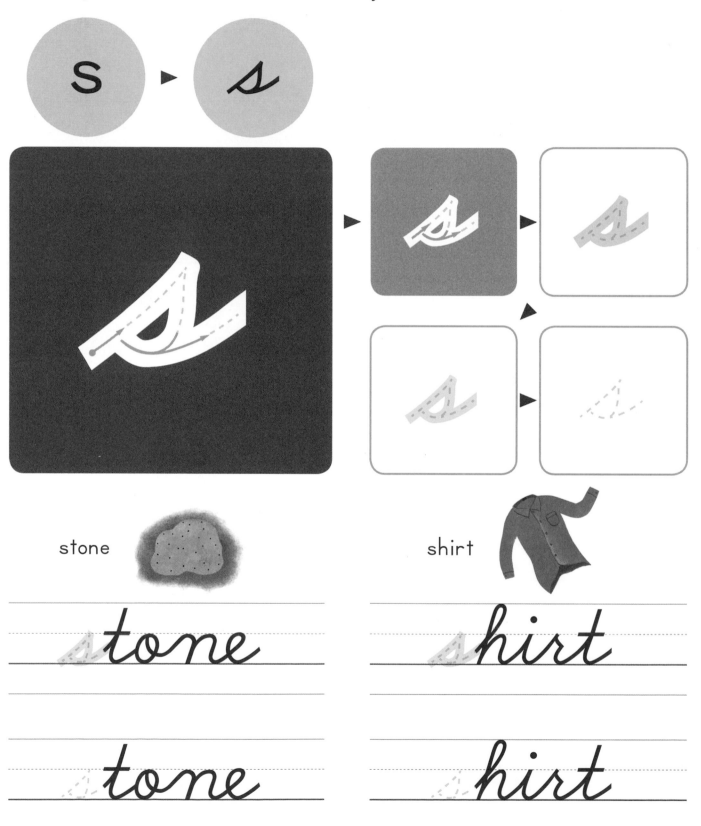

stone

shirt

Lowercase Letters

Writing v

Name

Date

■ Say the sound of the letter as you trace it. Then read the words aloud, and say the sound of the first letter as you trace it.

v ▶ v

van

vest

van

$vest$

van

$vest$

Review Writing *b*, *s*, and *v*

■ Read the words aloud, then say the sound of the letter as you trace it.

bat
bat

stone
stone

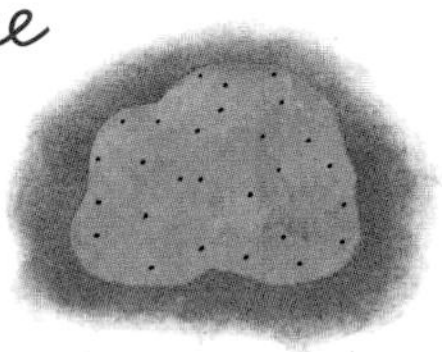

van
van

Lowercase Letters

Writing 𝓃

Name

Date

■ Say the sound of the letter as you trace it. Then read the words aloud, and say the sound of the first letter as you trace it.

n ▶ 𝓃

𝓃

nut

nose

𝓃𝓊𝓉

𝓃𝓸𝓈𝓮

𝓃𝓊𝓉

𝓃𝓸𝓈𝓮

Writing *m*

- Say the sound of the letter as you trace it. Then read the words aloud, and say the sound of the first letter as you trace it.

map

meat

map

map

meat

meat

Lowercase Letters

Writing *z*

Name

Date

■ Say the sound of the letter as you trace it. Then read the words aloud, and say the sound of the first letter as you trace it.

z ▶ *z*

zebra

zebra

ebra

zoo

zoo

oo

Review Writing *n*, *m*, and *z*

■ Read the words aloud, then say the sound of the letter as you trace it.

nut
nut

map
map

zebra
zebra

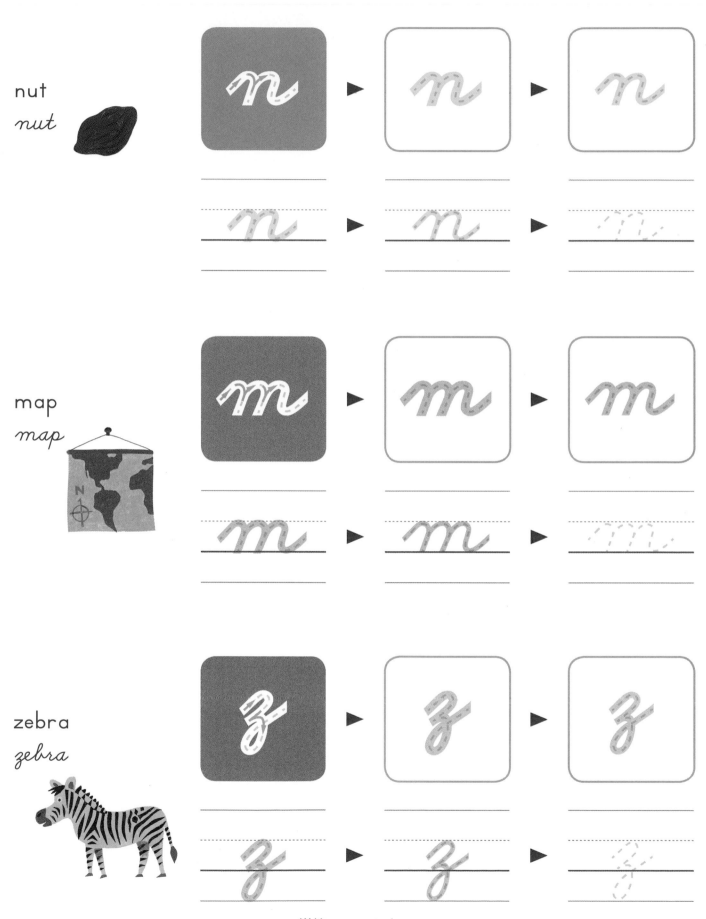

Lowercase Letters

Writing x

■ Say the sound of the letter as you trace it. Then read the words aloud, and say the sound of the first letter as you trace it.

X ▶ x

box

fox

box

fox

bo

fo

Writing *r*

■ Say the sound of the letter as you trace it. Then read the words aloud, and say the sound of the first letter as you trace it.

rooster

rabbit

Review

Writing *x* and *r*

Date

■ Read the words aloud, then say the sound of the letter as you trace it.

box
box

rooster
rooster

Writing *x* and *r*

35

Review   Writing *a-z*

■ Trace the letters a to z. Say the sound of the letter as you trace it.

Uppercase Letters

Writing *C*

Name

Date

■ Say the sound of the letter as you trace it. Then read the words aloud, and say the sound of the first letter as you trace it.

To parents

From this page on your child will learn cursive uppercase letters. Before your child begins writing the first letter of the words, please ask him or her to read the words. Encourage your child to write the letters carefully and say the sound of the letter aloud while he or she traces it. When your child completes each exercise, praise him or her.

C ▸ C

Can

Coat

Can

an

Coat

oat

Writing *a*

■Say the sound of the letter as you trace it. Then read the words aloud, and say the sound of the first letter as you trace it.

Ant

Apple

Ant

Apple

Ant

Apple

 **Uppercase Letters**

Writing O

Name

Date

■ Say the sound of the letter as you trace it. Then read the words aloud, and say the sound of the first letter as you trace it.

Ox

Octopus

Ox

Octopus

Review Writing C, a, and O

■Read the words aloud, then say the sound of the letter as you trace it.

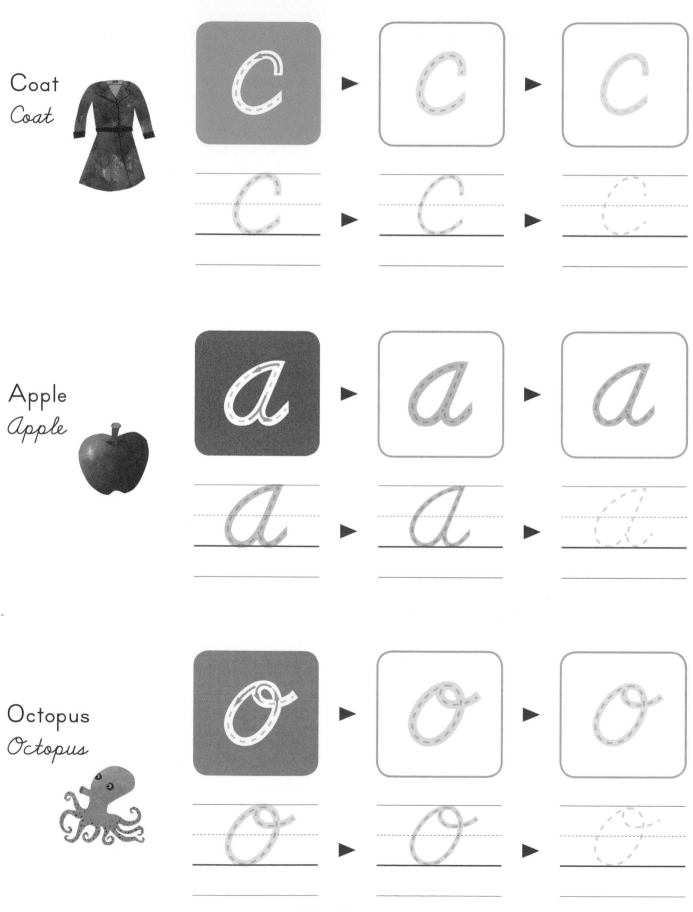

Coat
Coat

Apple
Apple

Octopus
Octopus

Uppercase Letters

Writing $\mathcal{U}$

Name

Date

▪Say the sound of the letter as you trace it. Then read the words aloud, and say the sound of the first letter as you trace it.

U ▸ $\mathcal{U}$

Up

Unicorn

$\mathcal{Up}$

$\mathcal{Up}$

$\mathcal{Unicorn}$

$\mathcal{Unicorn}$

Writing *W*

■ Say the sound of the letter as you trace it. Then read the words aloud, and say the sound of the first letter as you trace it.

Wink

Wet

Uppercase Letters

Writing $\mathcal{Y}$

Name

Date

■ Say the sound of the letter as you trace it. Then read the words aloud, and say the sound of the first letter as you trace it.

Y ▶ $\mathcal{Y}$

Yak

Yum

Review Writing *U*, *W*, and *Y*

■ Read the words aloud, then say the sound of the letter as you trace it.

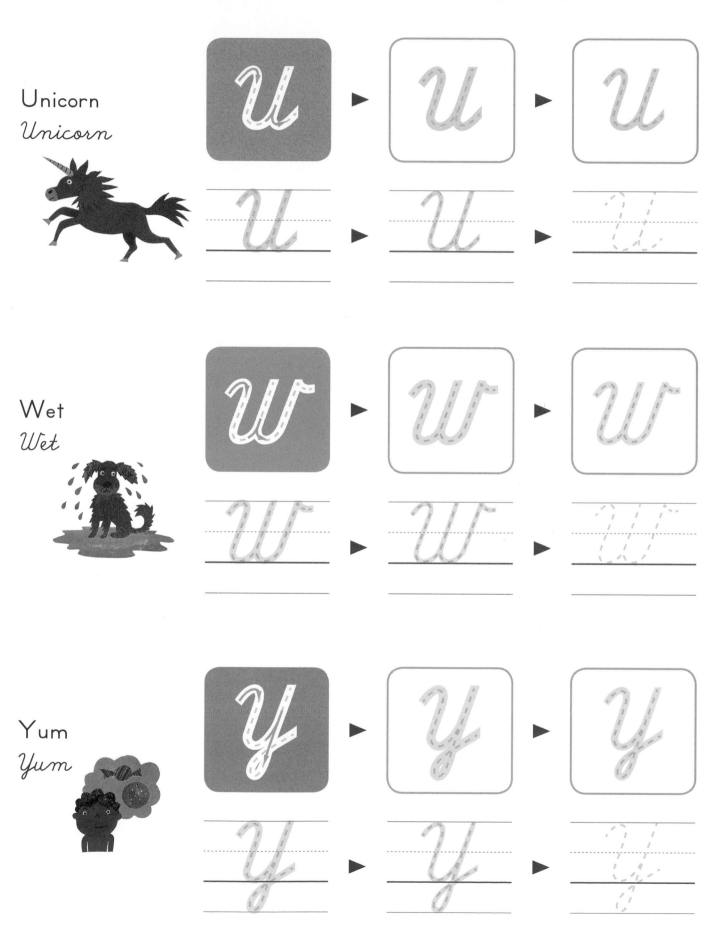

Unicorn
Unicorn

Wet
Wet

Yum
Yum

23 Uppercase Letters

Writing n

■ Say the sound of the letter as you trace it. Then read the words aloud, and say the sound of the first letter as you trace it.

N ▶ n

Nut

Nose

Nut

Nut

Nose

Nose

Writing *m*

■ Say the sound of the letter as you trace it. Then read the words aloud, and say the sound of the first letter as you trace it.

Map

Meat

Map

Meat

Map

Meat

Name

Date

■ Say the sound of the letter as you trace it. Then read the words aloud, and say the sound of the first letter as you trace it.

Z ▶ *Z*

Zebra

Zebra

ebra

Zoo

Zoo

oo

Review Writing *n*, *m*, and *z*

■ Read the words aloud, then say the sound of the letter as you trace it.

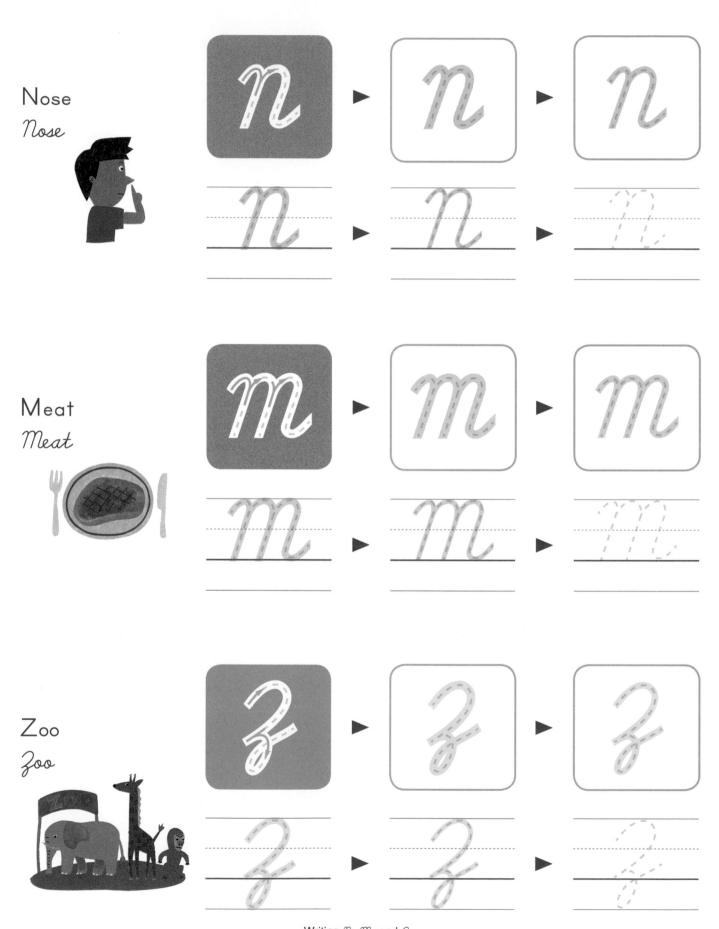

Nose
Nose

Meat
Meat

Zoo
Zoo

Uppercase Letters

Writing P

■ Say the sound of the letter as you trace it. Then read the words aloud, and say the sound of the first letter as you trace it.

Plane

Panda

Plane

Panda

Plane

Panda

Writing $\mathcal{R}$

■Say the sound of the letter as you trace it. Then read the words aloud, and say the sound of the first letter as you trace it.

Rooster

Rooster

Rooster

Rabbit

Rabbit

Rabbit

Uppercase Letters
Writing *B*

■ Say the sound of the letter as you trace it. Then read the words aloud, and say the sound of the first letter as you trace it.

Bat

Bag

Review Writing *P*, *R*, and *B*

▪ Read the words aloud, then say the sound of the letter as you trace it.

Panda
Panda

Rabbit
Rabbit

Bag
Bag

Uppercase Letters
Writing $\mathcal{V}$

Name

Date

■ Say the sound of the letter as you trace it. Then read the words aloud, and say the sound of the first letter as you trace it.

V ▶ $\mathcal{V}$

Van

Vest

$\mathcal{V}an$

$\mathcal{V}est$

$\mathcal{V}an$

$\mathcal{V}est$

Writing $\mathcal{V}$

53

Writing x

■Say the sound of the letter as you trace it. Then read the words aloud, and say the sound of the first letter as you trace it.

X-ray

Xylem

X-ray

Xylem

-ray

ylem

Uppercase Letters

Writing $\mathcal{K}$

Name

Date

■ Say the sound of the letter as you trace it. Then read the words aloud, and say the sound of the first letter as you trace it.

Kite

Knee

Review Writing $\mathcal{V}$, $\mathcal{X}$, and $\mathcal{K}$

■Read the words aloud, then say the sound of the letter as you trace it.

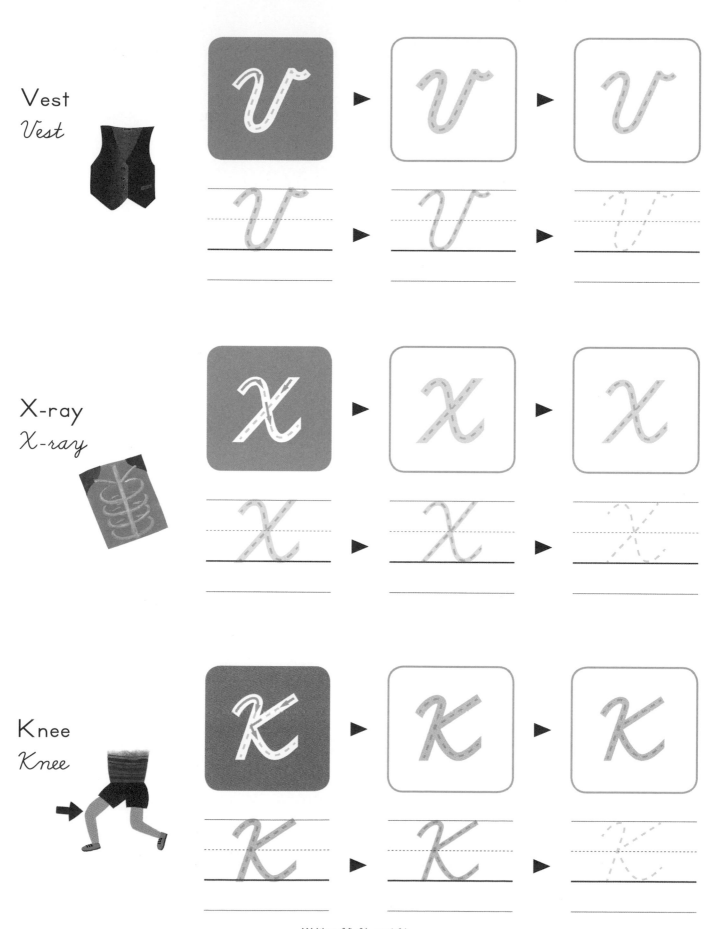

Vest
Vest

X-ray
X-ray

Knee
Knee

Uppercase Letters

Writing $\mathcal{T}$

Name

Date

■Say the sound of the letter as you trace it. Then read the words aloud, and say the sound of the first letter as you trace it.

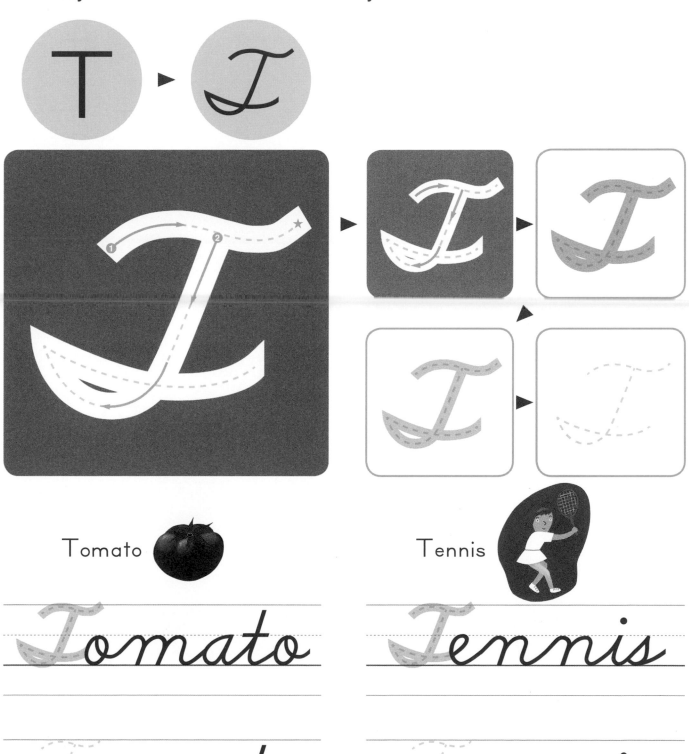

Tomato

Tennis

$\mathcal{T}$omato

$\mathcal{T}$ennis

$\mathcal{T}$omato

$\mathcal{T}$ennis

Writing *F*

■ Say the sound of the letter as you trace it. Then read the words aloud,
  and say the sound of the first letter as you trace it.

Flute

Flag

Uppercase Letters

Writing 𝓗

Name

Date

■Say the sound of the letter as you trace it. Then read the words aloud, and say the sound of the first letter as you trace it.

Hippo

Hose

Hippo

Hose

ippo

ose

Writing 𝓗

Review Writing 𝓘, 𝓕, and 𝓗

■ Read the words aloud, then say the sound of the letter as you trace it.

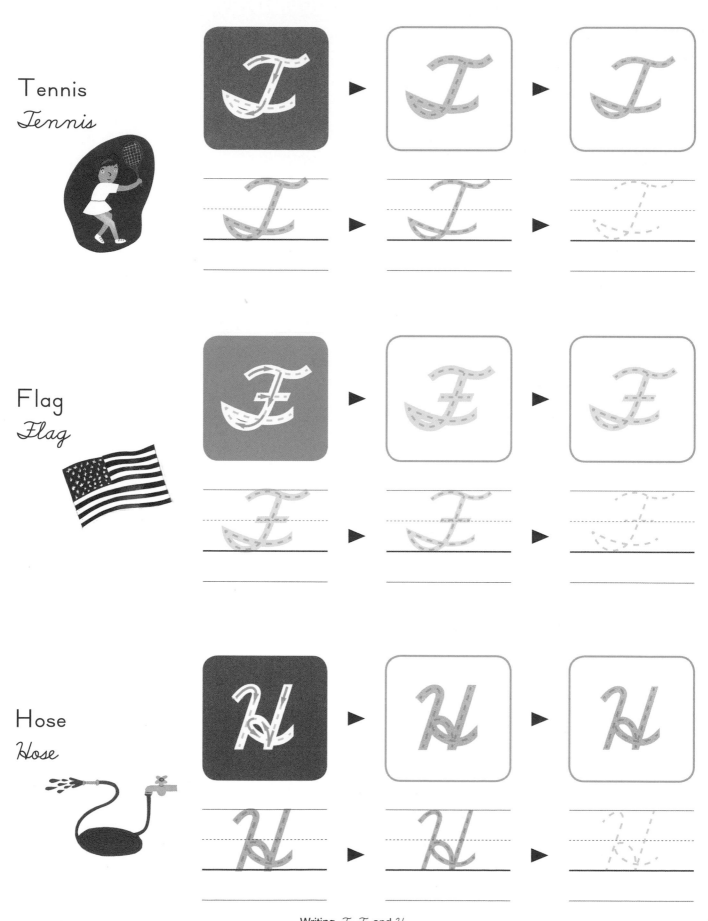

Tennis
Tennis

Flag
Flag

Hose
Hose

Uppercase Letters

Writing $\mathcal{L}$

Name

Date

■ Say the sound of the letter as you trace it. Then read the words aloud, and say the sound of the first letter as you trace it.

Lemon

Lamp

Writing $\mathcal{D}$

■Say the sound of the letter as you trace it. Then read the words aloud, and say the sound of the first letter as you trace it.

Doll

Dog

32 Uppercase Letters

Writing $\mathcal{J}$

Name
Date

■Say the sound of the letter as you trace it. Then read the words aloud, and say the sound of the first letter as you trace it.

Jacket

Jump

Jacket

acket

Jump

ump

Review Writing *L*, *D*, and *J*

■Read the words aloud, then say the sound of the letter as you trace it.

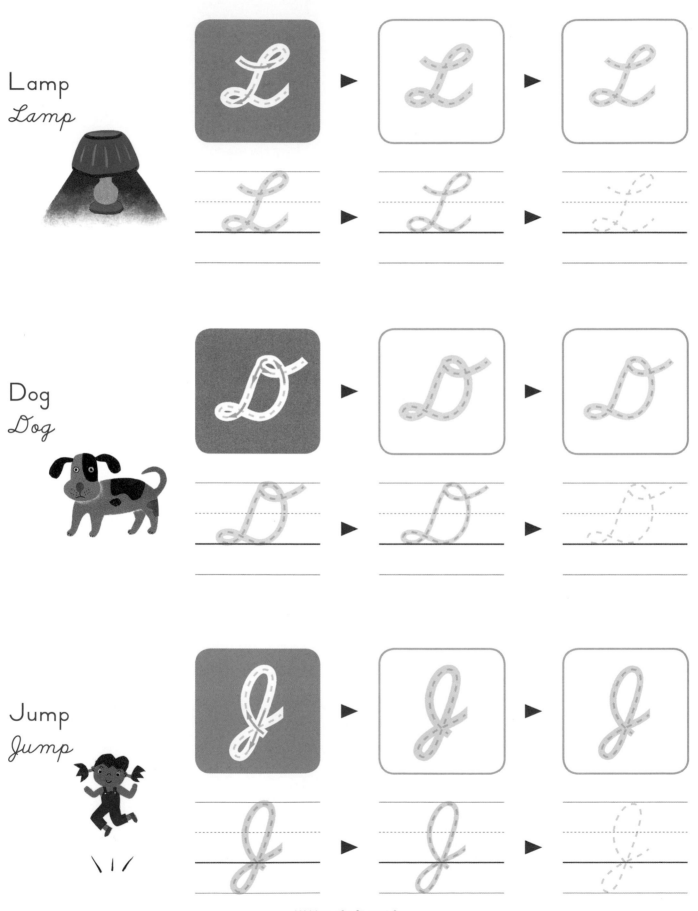

Lamp
Lamp

Dog
Dog

Jump
Jump

Name

Date

■ Say the sound of the letter as you trace it. Then read the words aloud, and say the sound of the first letter as you trace it.

Quail

Queen

Quail

Queen

Quail

Queen

Writing *I*

■ Say the sound of the letter as you trace it. Then read the words aloud, and say the sound of the first letter as you trace it.

Iguana

Ink

Uppercase Letters

Writing $\mathcal{E}$

■ Say the sound of the letter as you trace it. Then read the words aloud, and say the sound of the first letter as you trace it.

Egg

Elephant

$\mathcal{E}gg$

$\mathcal{E}lephant$

gg

$lephant$

Review Writing 𝒬, ℐ, and ℰ

■Read the words aloud, then say the sound of the letter as you trace it.

Queen
Queen

Ink
Ink

Elephant
Elephant

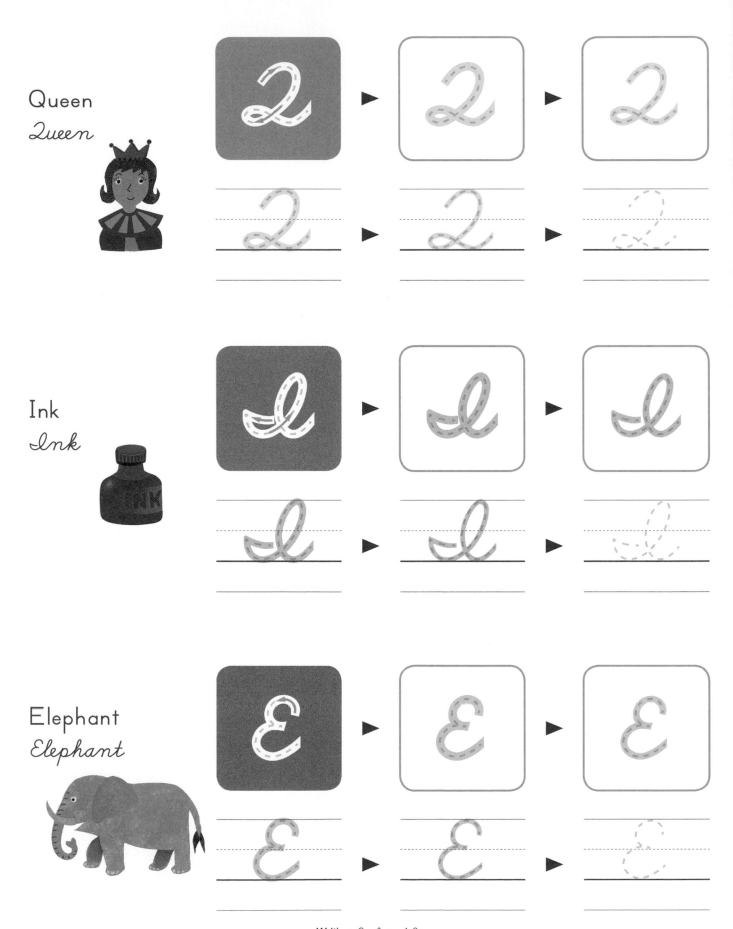

Uppercase Letters

Writing $\mathcal{G}$

■ Say the sound of the letter as you trace it. Then read the words aloud, and say the sound of the first letter as you trace it.

Gum

Goat

Writing *S*

■ Say the sound of the letter as you trace it. Then read the words aloud, and say the sound of the first letter as you trace it.

Stone

Shirt

Stone

Shirt

tone

hirt

Name
Date

■ Read the words aloud, then say the sound of the letter as you trace it.

Goat
Goat

Shirt
Shirt

Review Writing 𝑎-𝑧

■ Trace the letters A to Z. Say the sound of the letter as you trace it.

A ___    B ___    C ___    D ___

E ___    F ___    G ___    H ___

I ___    J ___    K ___    L ___

M ___    N ___    O ___    P ___

Q ___    R ___    S ___ 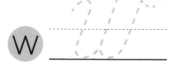   T ___

U ___    V ___ 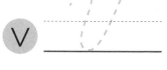   W ___   X ___

Y ___ 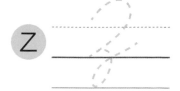   Z ___

Review
Writing *a - z*

Name
Date

- Trace the letters a to z. Say the sound of the letter as you trace it.

(a) _____   (b) _____   (c) _____   (d) _____

(e) _____   (f) _____   (g) _____   (h) _____

(i) _____   (j) _____   (k) _____   (l) _____

(m) _____   (n) _____   (o) _____   (p) _____

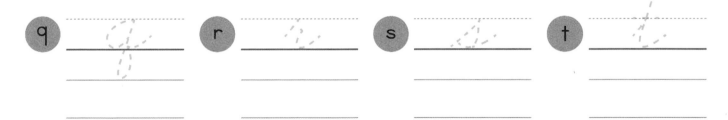

(q) _____   (r) _____   (s) _____   (t) _____

(u) _____   (v) _____   (w) _____   (x) _____

(y) _____   (z) _____

Writing *a - z*

To parents
There are no lines on this page to trace. It is okay if your child does not write each letter perfectly. When your child is finished, offer lots of praise.

■ Write the letters a to z, as shown on the left.

a _____   *b* _____   *c* _____   *d* _____

e _____   *f* _____   *g* _____   *h* _____

i _____   *j* _____   *k* _____   *l* _____

m _____   *n* _____   *o* _____   *p* _____

q _____   *r* _____   *s* _____   *t* _____

u _____   *v* _____   *w* _____   *x* _____

y _____   *z* _____

Review

Writing 𝒶-𝓏

Name	
Date	

■Trace the letters A to Z. Say the sound of the letter as you trace it.

Ⓐ _____ Ⓑ _____ Ⓒ _____ Ⓓ _____

Ⓔ _____ Ⓕ _____ Ⓖ _____ Ⓗ _____

Ⓘ _____ Ⓙ _____ Ⓚ _____ Ⓛ _____

Ⓜ _____ Ⓝ _____ Ⓞ _____ Ⓟ _____

Ⓠ _____ Ⓡ _____ Ⓢ _____ Ⓣ _____

Ⓤ _____ Ⓥ _____ Ⓦ _____ Ⓧ _____

Ⓨ _____ Ⓩ _____

Writing a-z

■Write the letters A to Z, as shown on the left.

a _____

B _____

C _____

D _____

E _____

F _____

G _____

H _____

I _____

J _____

K _____

L _____

m _____

n _____

O _____

P _____

2 _____

R _____

S _____

T _____

U _____

V _____

W _____

X _____

y _____

z _____

Name

Date

■ Write the letters A to Z, as shown on the left.

a _____ *B* _____ *C* _____ *D* _____

E _____ *F* _____ *G* _____ *H* _____

I _____ *J* _____ *K* _____ *L* _____

m _____ *n* _____ *O* _____ *P* _____

2 _____ *R* _____ *S* _____ *T* _____

U _____ *V* _____ *W* _____ *X* _____

y _____ *Z* _____

Writing *a-z*

■ Write the letters a to z, as shown on the left.

a _____   b _____   c _____   d _____

e _____   f _____   g _____   h _____

i _____   j _____   k _____   l _____

m _____   n _____   o _____   p _____

q _____   r _____   s _____   t _____

u _____   v _____   w _____   x _____

y _____   z _____

KUM◯N

Certificate of Achievement

is hereby congratulated on completing

My Book of CURSIVE WRITING: LETTERS

Presented on _____ , 20 ____

_____
Parent or Guardian